Cheyenne Tipi
Notes

Books by the author

Equine

The Natural Horse: Lessons from the Wild (1992)
Horse Owners Guide to Natural Hoof Care (1999)
Founder — Prevention and Cure the Natural Way (2001)
Guide To Booting Horses for Hoof Care Professionals (2002)
Paddock Paradise: A Guide to Natural Horse Boarding (2005)
The Natural Trim: Principles and Practice (2012)
The Healing Angle: Nature's Gateway to the Healing Field (2014)
Laminitis: An Equine Plague of Unconscionable Proportions (2016)
Training Manual: ISNHCP Natural Trim Training Program (2017)
The Natural Trim: Basic Guidelines (2019)
The Natural Trim: Advanced Guidelines (2019)

Other:

The Canvas Tipi (1982)
Guard Your Teeth: Why the Dental Industry Fails Us — A Guide to Natural Dental Care (2018)
Buckskin Tanner: A Guide to Natural Hide Tanning (2019)
Cheyenne Tipi Notes (1903): Technical Insights Into 19th Century Plains Indian Bison Hide Tanning (2019)
Zoo Paradise: A New Model for Humane Zoological Gardens (2019)

Cheyenne Tipi Notes

Technical Insights Into 19th Century Plains Indian Bison Hide Tanning

A Detailed Description
by Ethnographer James Mooney
of Southern Cheyenne Women
Tanning Cow Hides For A
Historic Reproduction
of A 19th Century Hide Tipi
April 28th – June 2nd, 1903
Darlington Indian Agency
Oklahoma Territory

Transcription of Mooney Notes by

Jaime Jackson
Author, *Buckskin Tanner*

Natural World Publications

©2019 Jaime Jackson

Contact the author at:
Natural World Publications
P.O. Box 1765
Harrison, AR 72602
jacksonaanhcp@gmail.com

Other written works by the author:
www.NaturalWorldPublications.com

Cheyenne Tipi Notes
ISBN-13: 978-1-7333094-0-0

Contents

Preface: Historical Notes	*6*
Introduction	*10*
Transcription Key	*13*
Page 1 "Hide Dressing"	*15*
Page 2 "Dressing"	*17*
Page 3 "Hides"	*19*
Page 4 "Hides"	*21*
Page 5 "Hides"	*23*
Page 6 "Hides"	*25*
Postscript	*26*
Image credits	*29*
Buckskin Tanner	*30*
About the Author	*31*

Preface: Historical Notes

One may ask why would James Mooney (1861-1921), an American ethnologist, encourage Cheyenne Indians at the turn of the 19th century to recreate an authentic Plains Indian tipi made of hides? When not a generation before the United States military did everything it could to destroy entire tipi villages in a protracted effort to break down the backbone of Plains Indian culture and compel assimilation into the encroaching American civilization? History has shown that post Civil War American expansionism in the west was inevitable. But at the same time, militant Indian tribes with horsed warriors in the thousands across the plains, were equally determined not to give up their lands and ways without a fight. In the end, however, sheer numbers of U.S. soldiers with superior military and industrial might — if not unknown to recalcitrant tribes, certainly was not completely understood — brought tragic deaths, chaos, bitter defeat, and ultimately submission across the plains tribes. They were to give up their Plains Indian lifestyle, including their conical homes, and accept their fate. In spite of this unsettling backdrop, Mooney and the Cheyenne understood the importance of saving as much of their culture for posterity as possible. And so the tipi project went forward.

Given the gravity of the historical context in which it happened, such an endeavor speaks volumes to the strength of character and foresight of both Mooney and the Cheyenne. To me, the obscure story behind this tipi — in particular, how the tipi's hides were tanned, which is the primary focus of this book — is worth sharing, especially with today's international legions of tipi and Indian tanning enthusiasts who are carrying on the Plains Indian and frontier traditions of the past.

Tipis created from bison hides fell not only from the "scorched earth" military tactics borne of the Civil War and then systematically deployed by Army Generals against the tribes, their lodges, and their horse herds, but from the eradication of the vast bison herds themselves. Millions of free-roaming bison, the target of a burgeoning American commerce hungering for their hides, meat, and bones, faced their own native demise, dwindling into mere hundreds by the time Mooney arrived among the Cheyenne in the late 1800s. With the bison resource for their survival depleted, coupled to a string of broken treaties orchestrated by a corrupt U.S. Congress compelling them to unconditionally vacate their lands and lodges, as well as increasing numbers of settlers now demanding Indian lands, and the incessant U.S. military pressure to do as they're told "or else," the southern bands of Cheyenne and their tribal compatriots, the Arapaho, soon found themselves confined to reservation lands in what would become just a few years later the State of Oklahoma.

Preface: Historical Notes

In the 16th century, 25–30 million bison (also called buffalo) inhabited North America. As a species, they were hunted almost to extinction in the 19th century. Less than 600 remained in the wild by the late 1880s, although some historians think possibly less than 100. (*Top*) Rath & Wright's buffalo hide yard in Dodge City, Kansas, showing 40,000 stacked bison hides. (*Bottom*) 1892: bison skulls await industrial processing at Michigan Carbon Works in Rogueville (a suburb of Detroit). Bones were processed to be used for glue, fertilizer, dye/tint/ink, or were burned to create "bone char" which was an important component for sugar refining. Destruction of the bison herds spelled doom for the Plains Indian culture.

Arapaho tipi village, 1868. The Cheyenne and Arapaho signed the Fort Laramie Treaty with the U.S. in 1851. It recognized and guaranteed their rights to traditional lands in portions of Colorado, Kansas, Nebraska, and Wyoming. The U.S. could not enforce the treaty, however, and European-American trespassers overran Indian lands. There were repeated conflicts between settlers and members of the tribes. Following the Medicine Lodge Treaty of 1867, Cheyenne and Arapaho bands, either from force or seeking protection from American military forces, began their relocation to their new homes in the Indian Territory (now the State of Oklahoma). Congressional "plenary powers" accorded by the U.S. Supreme court in 1903, stripped nearly all treaty lands from all Indian tribes.

Mooney was fully aware of the devastation of Plains Indian culture and what surviving Cheyenne related to him as the "old ways." Unlike hostile and arguably corrupt congressional forces who wanted the Cheyenne to give up their ways and get on with their assimilation into the American way, Mooney genuinely appreciated their culture and implored the Cheyenne to work with him to preserve it as much as possible for posterity's sake. This included creating a hide tipi representative of a Cheyenne home before their relocation to Indian Territory in the late 1860s and 70s. But Mooney first had to convince his bureaucratic seniors at the Bureau of Ethnology and the Smithsonian Institution, and also leery congressional oversight committees who could fund his project, that it had merit. His plan was to enter the tipi and other items at the 1904 St. Louis Exposition, after which it would find a permanent home in the Field Columbian Museum in Chicago. Mooney skillfully played his hand, convincing his overseers it was a good idea because the exposition needed material representation of extinguished "primitive cultures" as proof of their inferiority and the justification for their subjugation, eradication, and replacement by modern civilization. That did it. Mooney got the money and the go ahead. Indian agents at the Darlington Indian Agency and military forces garrisoned at nearby Ft. Reno (the Cheyenne and Arapaho were still under military supervision) would stand down, cooperate and allow the project to go forth.

Hide tanning and tipi construction was the work of Cheyenne women. Elder Cheyenne women trained to do this work fifty years earlier by an earlier generation, were still alive and knowledgeable. Mooney convinced them to guide the process from "rawhide to tipi," to which they consented. Once organized, the tanning project took a little over a month, concluding in June of 1903. Construction of the tipi and other items of cultural significance then followed. A year later, Mooney invited journalists and other civilians, military figures from nearby Fort Reno, and local Cheyenne tribal members, to visit the finished tipi. Included below by way of concluding this preface, is the report of one journalist in attendance for his Chicago newspaper, published 115 years ago:

"James Mooney has been working among the Cheyenne Indians in Oklahoma all this winter building this tepee. It will correspond in every detail with the typical home of a Cheyenne warrior of fifty years ago. The purpose in building this tepee is to preserve permanently the truest type of a North American Indian home. The Cheyenne are losing their knowledge of old days and old ways so rapidly that Prof. Mooney was asked to undertake the work before it was too late.

"The tepee stands in the yard of the old frontier hotel at Darlington, which Prof. Mooney has rented from cellar to garret and occupied last winter as his field home and storehouse. At a distance of fifty feet the tepee appears to be built of heavy white duck [canvas], but closer inspection shows that the material is rawhide, tanned so soft that it can be rolled in the hand like a woolen blanket, and colored a rich creamy white.

"The Cheyenne women worked many weeks tanning the raw skins and used great quantities of beef liver, marrow and brains in their labor. The Indian home is cone-shaped and the skin covering is one single piece. Skill and experience are required in fashioning the irregularly shaped skins into a whole that shall be perfect in length and width. Sinew alone was used in sewing the skins together. The seams are as even as a tightly twisted cord and pressed till scarcely discernible in the uniform smoothness of the assembled skins. Rain and snow may fall and wind and dust gnaw at the stitches, but they will not break in a generation.

"The tepee is about eighteen feet in height, and about fifteen in diameter at the base, and faces the east, according to Indian religious custom. Prof. Mooney permitted the tepee to be inspected by strangers for the first time on New Year's day, and many handsome women and gold-braided officers came from the garrison at Fort Reno to see it. In spite of a roaring wind that came down from the north across the brown prairies they found the tepee surprisingly warm and comfortable. A small fire blazed cheerily in the hollow place scooped in the ground at the center, and the smoke went curling out at the opening at the top. White visitors stood around and sneezed and coughed and wiped involuntary tears from their cheeks, till Prof. Mooney said, 'Sit down on the seats and you will not be annoyed by the smoke.'

"Indian men, women, and children, both Cheyennes and Arapahoes, abandoned their usual stoicism to grin and point approvingly at the 'heap big fine tepee' which only that day had been erected by three or four squaws. Admiring Indians pushed their way into the tepee, made themselves at home, and enjoyed its magnificence and comfort. Many years had passed since its equal had been seen in Oklahoma, where the Indians grow poorer as the moons ride to the west." — Correspondent for the Chicago Daily News, 4/13/1904

Introduction

To the best of my knowledge this is the only transcription of James Mooney's six pages of notes on the tanning of cow (bovine) hides for a tipi in the spring/summer of 1903 by a dozen or so women of the southern branch of the Cheyenne nation.[1] Further, it appears also to be the only step by step accounting of any such tanning by 19th century Native Americans, where the tannage has survived into the present and is available for inspection. Historically, many early first hand accountings of Indian tanning have been published. But without exception the observers themselves were not tanners, and this is reflected in their descriptions, including Mooney's. But what is remarkably unique about Mooney's are their great detail, which, although not what we would expect from a literate and accomplished tanner to record in terms of tanning science and a highly technical methodology, they are 100 percent correlatable to the outcome — a hide tipi — preserved in a museum to this day. To natural tanning aficionados and others, Mooney's project was an incredibly significant contribution.

Background

As I've written in the preface, Mooney — an ethnographer employed by the Smithsonian Institution's Bureau of Ethnology on both sides of the 1900th millennial — sought to preserve accurate representation of Indian culture. This, at a time when the U.S. Government was reluctant to fund any "Indian research" that didn't have sufficient usefulness to be justified. Congress, having already funded a costly and protracted war against Indian tribes across the Great Plains, and then having to fund numerous reservations incarcerating tens of thousands of Indians defeated in battle, was in no mood to dole out yet more money to "preserve tipi culture" it had just extinguished militarily and wanted Indians to have no more to do with. But Mooney cleverly convinced stubborn Smithsonian bureaucrats, themselves answerable to the purse string holders in Congress, to push for the project to go forward on the basis of two convincing arguments.

---

[1] I completed the transcription over several months during the winter of 1983–1984.

Introduction

The tipi could be displayed at the upcoming international 1904 St. Louis Exposition. Organizers had put together a racist panorama of "primitive peoples" from around the world, providing purported evidence for millions of gawking visitors from around the world of civilized peoples superiority. And then soon afterward, the tipi would be given a permanent home at the prestigious Chicago Columbian Field Museum to continue on as a muse for more gawkers. Ironically, the tipi, locked away in the museum's catacomb of confiscated Indian artifacts, hasn't seen the light of day in over a century with the exception of one or two brief "outings."

At the same time, Mooney had to convince the Southern Cheyenne to make the tipi, when they themselves were struggling with poverty and reeling from the unsettling pressure of the "1892 Land Run" on Cheyenne and Arapaho treaty lands. Fortunately, on both accounts, Mooney succeeded.

Tipi hide-tanning notes

Mooney's notoriously terrible handwriting, which infected all his research notes in the field, was legend in his day and into the present. It especially irritated his bureaucratic handlers at the Smithsonian who insisted he spend more time out of the field transcribing his own notes so that others could read them. When I first discovered the tipi notes, embedded in 75 pages of Mooney's "Miscellaneous notes on the Cheyenne. 1903–1906," I was shocked. How could anyone read them, let alone make sense of them? I sought out anthropologists familiar with Mooney who, by some miracle, may have transcribed all of his Cheyenne notes. To my dismay, the six pages dealing with the tanning were what they all avoided, but with good reason. First, beyond their illegibility, the notes are difficult to follow even if one is an experienced natural tanner. Had Mooney followed the tanning sequences of one or just a few hides, the pages would have been much more useful as a study in Cheyenne tanning. But because Mooney was clearly struggling to keep up with the Cheyenne tanners, and represent their work in an orderly manner, the reader must also try to figure out the tanning sequences in which 27 hides were processed! Mooney probably did the best he could under the circumstances. It would have been a struggle for anyone.

It took me months to set up an alphabetic transcription key, identifying letters in the few word spellings of Mooney's that were "relatively" obvious. From this letter base, I ventured into the six pages of his calligraphy to identify letters wherever they might be found. As words began to emerge, the letter base expanded. However, I soon realized that Mooney took liberty with abbreviations of words, if not phrases, as he probably never gave a thought to someone having to read or study them or his notes. Eventually, what began to immerge was something tantamount to the "puzzle board" on the TV program "Wheel of Fortune." My job was to somehow fill in the blanks based on what was known and what I knew about tanning. This was tough as here and there Mooney sprinkled the text with a smattering of Cheyenne terms, which had to be weeded out. Fortunately, the language of "natural tanning" crosses many cultural lines and I began to see the common threads in terms of method and materials. Eventually, I was able to transcribe almost all of his notes. But more important, enough that I could see clearly what the Cheyenne women were doing. I had busted the "Mooney Code."

The Cheyenne tipi

But the transcribed notes were not enough, as Mooney himself had no thought to using comparative tannage to provide additional nuance to his transcription. Not even my extensive experience as a tanner was enough to detect this from his notes. It was clear I needed to see the Cheyenne tipi to confirm what my experience and intuition had by then led me to understand regarding bison (bovine) hide tanning. I won't repeat the lengthy narrative here that led me physically to the tipi, what I discovered after I examined it, and how I successfully created bison buckskin, as it is all in my book, *Buckskin Tanner — A Guide to Natural Tanning*. What follows is my detailed transcription of Mooney's six pages of tanning notes. Additionally, where pertinent I've added my comments to provide further clarification to his notes. One such clarification is in order out front, however, to correct the Smithsonian's archival record.

The BAE catalogue file reads:

> Mooney, James. Miscellaneous notes on the Cheyenne. 1903–1906. Approx. 75 pp.

> Difficult script, but legible to reader familiar with Mooney's writing and abbreviations. Includes day-by-day account of hide-dressing process, April. 28—May 28, 1903. Corresponding snapshots by Mooney (somewhat blurred) are in BAE photographic files, 'original prints' series.

In fact, the tanning did not end until June 2, 1903 (see "Hides" [page 6]. But one would not know this unless they had cracked the Mooney Code themselves!

Transcription Key

[#] = Far left column are my line numbers, corresponding to sentences in Mooney's 6 pages of notes.

[?] = I'm not able to transcribe a word.

↙ = Arrows replace Mooney's lines, connecting sentence fragments and/or information across multiple lines.

[messages] = where it seems pertinent, I've inserted short messages to the reader within brackets to clarify transcription.

[footnote]^x = ^{x} refers reader to footnotes where I include commentary to further clarify Mooney's text.

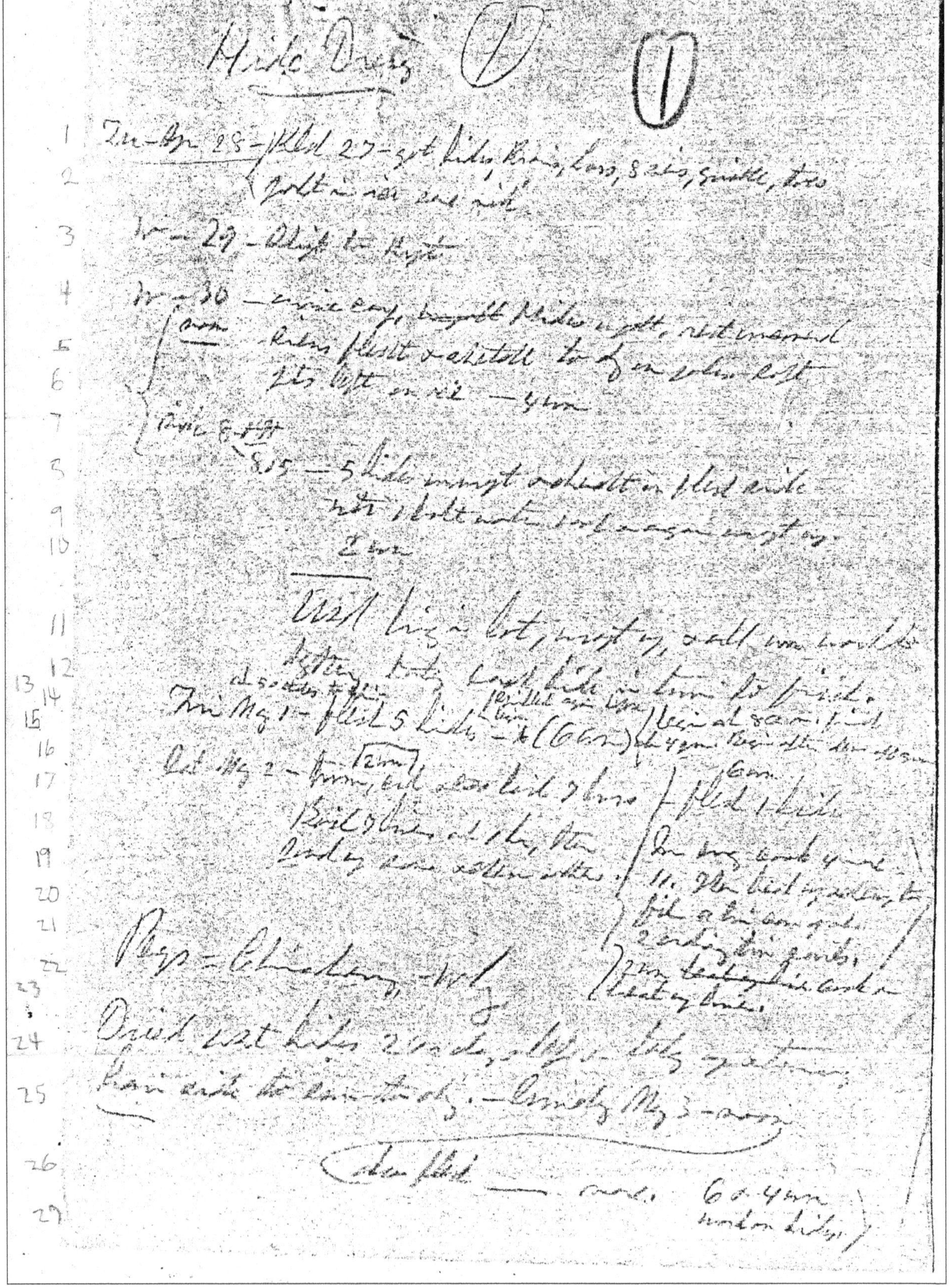

TRANSCRIPTION: PAGE 1

Hide Dressing I

Line
- [1] **Tuesday – April 28 –** killed 27 – Got hides, brains, livers, 8 sinews, gristle, toes.
- [2] Packed in ice and salt.
- [3] **Wednesday – 29th –** Ship to [?][1]
- [4] **Thursday – 30th –** Arrive in camp. hides wrapped, rest uncovered.
- [5] Noon — Sinew fleshed and stretched to dry on poles. Soft
- [6] parts left in ice — 4 women.
- [7] Night — 8 pm
- [8] 8:15 — 5 hides unwrapped and [salt?]) on flesh side.
- [9] [water?] 1 bucket of water soak & again wrapped up
- [10] 2 women.
- [11] Thursday bring in lot, wrapped up, & all women worked
- [12] together staking each hide in time to finish
- [13] at 50 stakes to hide sprinkled again before begin at 8 am. Finish
- [14] beginning[2] at 4 pm. Begin after ? ? ?
- [15] **Friday, May 1 –** Flesh 5 hides 6 women off ?
- [16] 2 women 6 women
- [17] **Saturday, May 2 –** trim, cut also boil 7 brains flesh 1 hide
- [18] boil 7 livers at 1 hour, stir in evening cook 4 more
- [19] lard up some, and stir often livers. Then heat up & soften to
- [20] fill a tin can of ?
- [21] 2 ? tin quarts.]
- [22] Pegs = clinching – working 2 women [scratched out text] cook &
- [23] heat up livers.
- [24] Dried 1st hides 2½ days before taking up & turning
- [25] hair side to face the sky. — **Sunday, May 3rd –** noon
- [26] to flesh 6[3] more. 6 + 4 women
- [27] work on hides.

---

[1] Mooney indicates shipping everything to the tanning camp. However, his notes are not legible enough to say where this is precisely located. But as the finished tipi was eventually displayed in what was the Darlington (Cheyenne and Arapaho) Indian Agency in the Oklahoma Territory near the military garrison of Ft. Reno, the Agency is one possibility. On the other hand, the Cheyenne and Arapaho by then had begun moving to Concho, Oklahoma, where the Darlington Agency was also relocated to in 1909 (and which today serves as their tribal headquarters). So, Concho is also a possibility, but less likely, it seems to me, as the bustling land rush town of El Reno and nearby Ft. Reno, would be more opportune sources of hides, which favors the Agency, or nearby. Mooney states on Page 4, Line 6, that he is going to town — this could be a reference to El Reno. Further, because his notes state that work also began on Wednesday, the proximity of the tanning site to the hide source would also seem to favor the Darlington Agency (or close by). But I am speculating, and other researchers may have more definitive information.

[2] I am assuming he means sprinkling with water.

[3] I moved 6 over to this position, rather than 10 women working on hides.

TRANSCRIPTION: PAGE 2

"Dressing 2"

[1]   2 women   (to soften hide)
[2] **Tuesday** cook brains, livers, and toes,[1] wait & mix together with 3 quarts lard, and little salt
[3]   in 1 pot   at 1 hour.
[4] Osage, Kansas, & Cheyenne in Eastern Oklahoma mix brains to dress robes ?, except on brain side
[5]   in robe grease & because
[6]   well blended[2]
[7]   keep out [?][3] of best fiber for brush to rub mixture in hide.
[8]   steer hide thicker & harder to work than cow hide, but makes more [? ? ?]
[9] Cold water stiffens skins & makes harder to dress.
[10]   Robes here not good until about mid-December. Matured earlier/ or not / in north &
[11]   had finer [buffalo?] hair. Coat on hides had more ground worms. Northern hides of any
[12]   animal better than south.
[13] [Cheyenne ——————————————————→][4]
[14]   because ? to mix with brains for ? ⟨liver = [?][4] , same word as for woman.
[15]   grease, lard, & [?][4] = [?][4]
[16]   [?][4], wash boil cook & pour into thick bags & let harden.

---

[1] I am assuming he means "hooves."
[2] Could also pass for "kneaded."
[3] A Cheyenne term?
[4] I believe this is a string of Cheyenne terms.

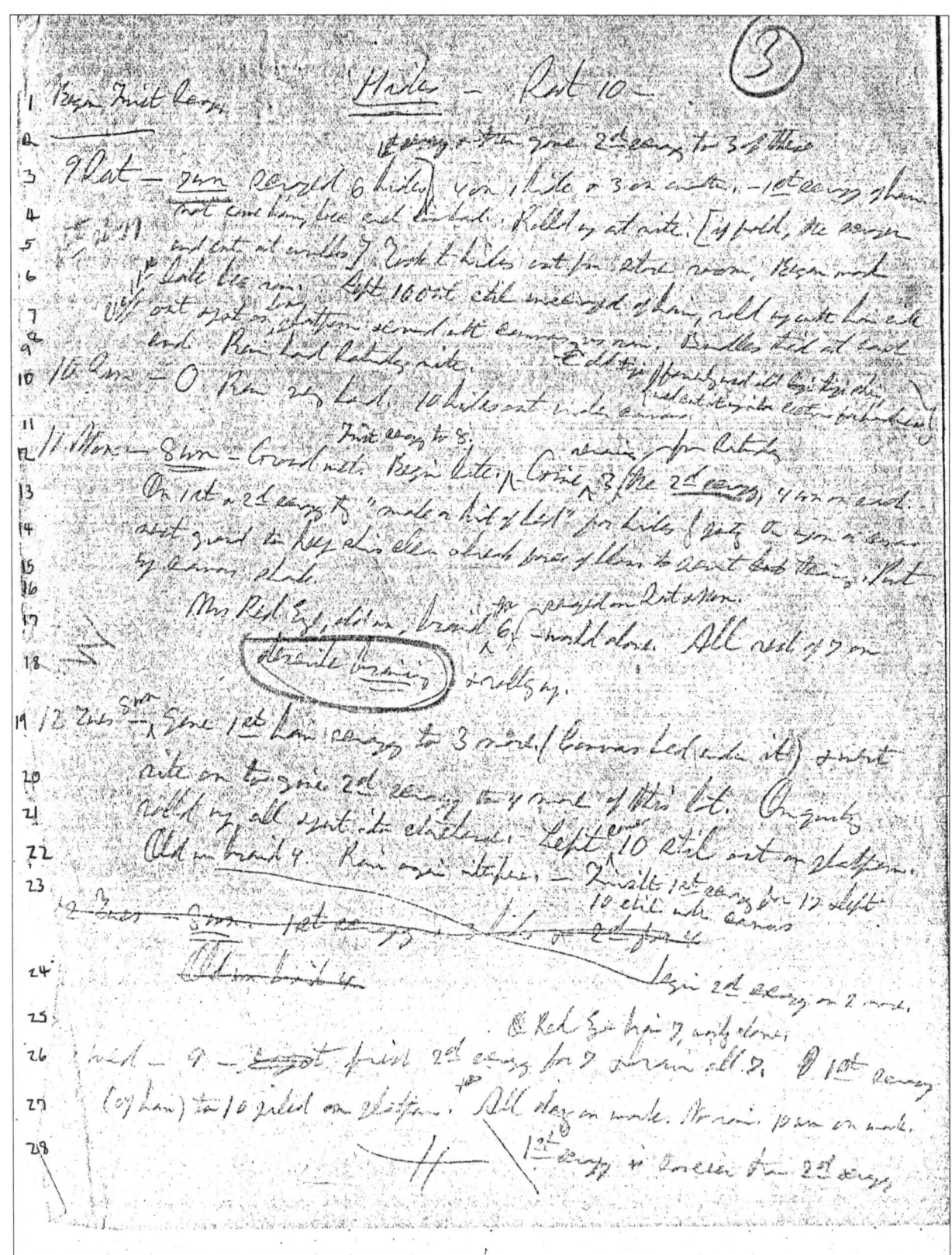

"Hides 3"

[1] Begin first scrape.
[2] 1st scraping & after give 2nd scraping to 3 of these
[3] **9th Saturday**—7 women scraped 6 hides, 4 on 1 hide & 3 on another—1st scraping off hair.
[4] not some hair, because ? ?. Rolled up at night {If folded, the scraper
[5] end cuts at wrinkles]. Took the hides out from store room. Began work
[6] 11:00 because rain. Left 10 out still unscraped of hair, roll up with hair side
[7] out & put long on platform & covered with canvas because [of] rain. Bundles tied at each
[8] end. Rains hard Saturday night.   old tipi /formerly used old tipi skin,
[9]   \used to cut it up into curtains for lodges. /
[10] **10th Sunday**   "0" [zero?] Rained very hard. 10 hides out under canvas.
[11]   First scraping to 8.   braining from Saturday.
[12] **11th Monday** – 8 women — ground wet.   Begin late.   Give 3 the 2nd scraping, 4 women on each.
[13]   On 1st & 2nd scraping try "make a kind of bed" for hides if dirty or canvas
[14]   next to ground to keep skins clean & break force of blow to prevent tearing. Put
[15]   up canvas shade.
[16]   the   scraped on Saturday and Monday.
[17]   Mrs. Red Eagle, old woman, brained 6   — worked alone.   All rest of 7 women
[18]   describe braining & rolling up.

[19] **12th Tuesday** – 8 women give 1st hair scraping to 3 more. (Canvas bed under it) & went
[20]   right on to give 2nd scraping to 4 more of this lot. On quitting
[21]   rolled up all & put into storehouse. Left some 10 still out on platform.
[22]   Old woman brained 4. Rained again — interferes. Finished 1st scraping for 17, & left
[23]   10 still under canvas.

[24]   ► began 2nd scraping on 2 more.
[25]   Red Eagle brained 7, working alone.
[26] **13th Wednesday** – 9 [hides?] — finish 2nd scraping for 7 & brain all 7. 1st scraping
[27]   (of hair) to 10 finished on platform. /All day in work. No rain. 10 women on work
[28]   \1st scraping is easier than 2nd scraping.

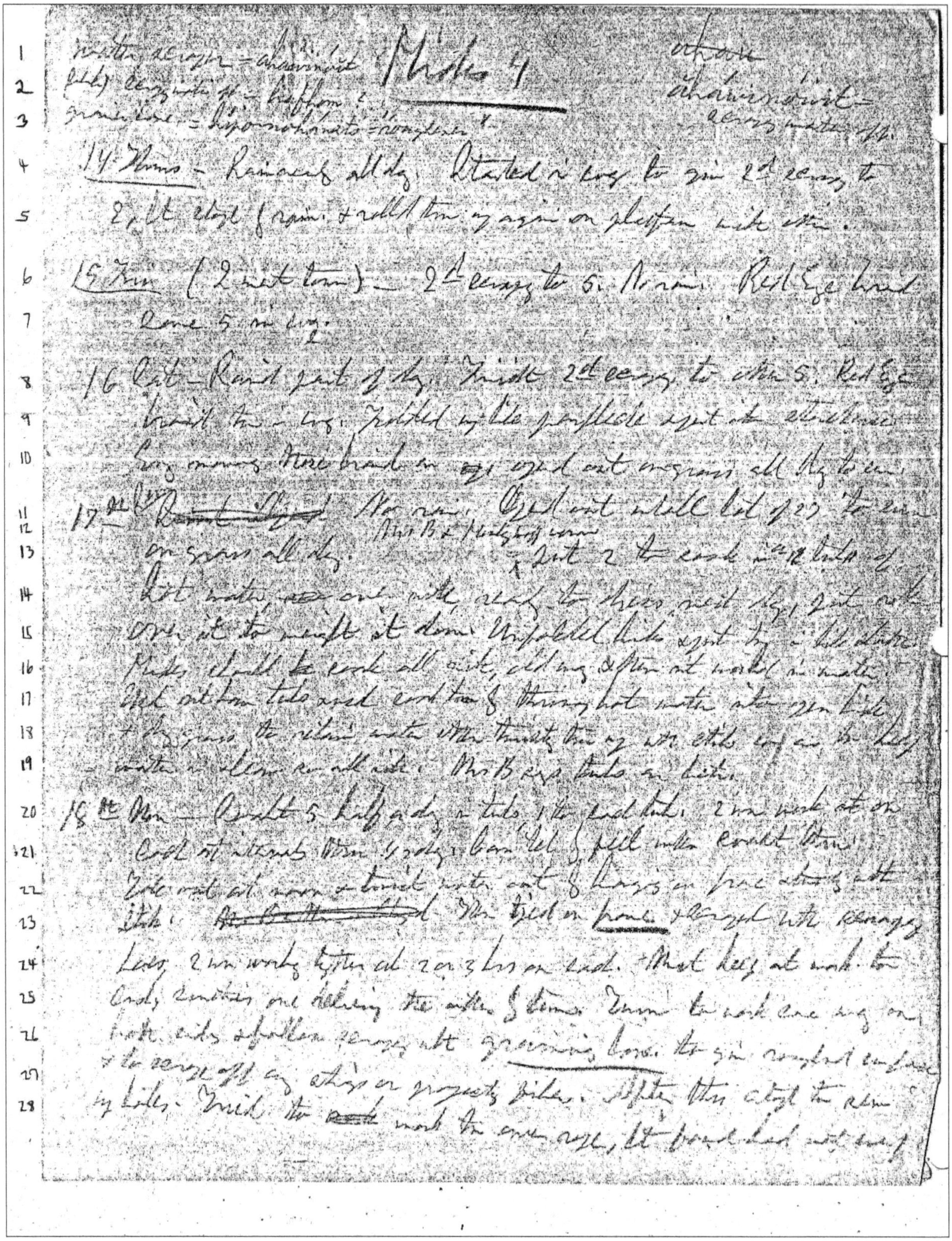

Notes 4

14 Thurs — Rained all day. Started in camp to give 2d scraping to 2, but stopped f[or] rain & rolled them up again on platform with others.

15 Fri (2 went to town) — 2d scraping to 5. No rain. Red Eye [illegible] Done 5 [illegible]

16 Sat — Rained part of day. Finished 2d scraping to other 5. Red Eye [illegible] [illegible] folded up the [illegible] [illegible]

17th [illegible] No rain. Opened out whole lot of 27 [illegible] on grass all day. Mrs B. & [illegible] came. Put 2 to soak in tubs of hot water, [illegible] ready to scrape next day, put rock over it to weight it down. Unfolded hides & put [illegible] [illegible] [illegible] [illegible] hot water [illegible] Mrs B [illegible]

18th Mon — [illegible] [illegible] [illegible] [illegible]

"Hides 4"

[1] Water scraper = [Cheyenne word]
[2] (stretch) scrape water off = [Cheyenne word]
[3] graining bone = [Cheyenne word] = [Cheyenne word]
[4] **14th Thursday [May]** – rains nearly all day. Started in evening to give 2nd scraping to
[5] 9, but stopped by rain. & rolled them up again on platform with others.
[6] **15th Friday** – (I went to town). – 2nd scraping to 5. No rain. Red Eagle brained
[7]   same 3 in evening.
[8] **16th Saturday** – Rained part of day. Finished 2nd scraping to other 5. Red Eagle
[9]   brained them in evening. Folded up like parfleche & put into storehouse
[10]   ? Evening moving those brained & opened out on grass all day to sun
[11] **17th Sunday** – No rain. Opened out whole lot of 27 to sun
[12]   (Mrs. B & Misty Wolf woman)
[13]   on grass all day.   Put 2 to soak in a tub of
[14]   hot water, over night, ready to dress next day, put rock
[15]   over it to weight it down. Unfolded hides & put in them on hide stretchers.
[16]   Hides should soak all night, old way, & then not worked in water.
[17]   Used [?] low tubs & use to soak them by throwing hot water into open hide
[18]   and dry grass to retain water & often twisting them up with sticks so as to help
[19]   water in & leave soak all night. Mrs. B says tubs are better.
[20] **18th Monday** – Soaked 5 half a day in tubs, 1 to each tub. 2 women work at one
[21]   both at intervals thru ½ day. Can tell by feeling when soaked through.
[22]   Take out at noon & twist water out of by hanging in frames & twisting with
[23]   stick. Then tied on frame & scraped with scraping
[24]   hoes. 2 women working together at 2 or 3 hours on each. Must keep at work to
[25]   end, sometimes one relieving the other by turns. Turned to work each way on
[26]   both sides & follow scraping with graining bone to give roughened surface
[27]   & to scrape off any strings or projecting fibers. After this stopped to remove
[28]   [?] hides. Tried to work them over rope, but found had not enough [cont'd page 5]

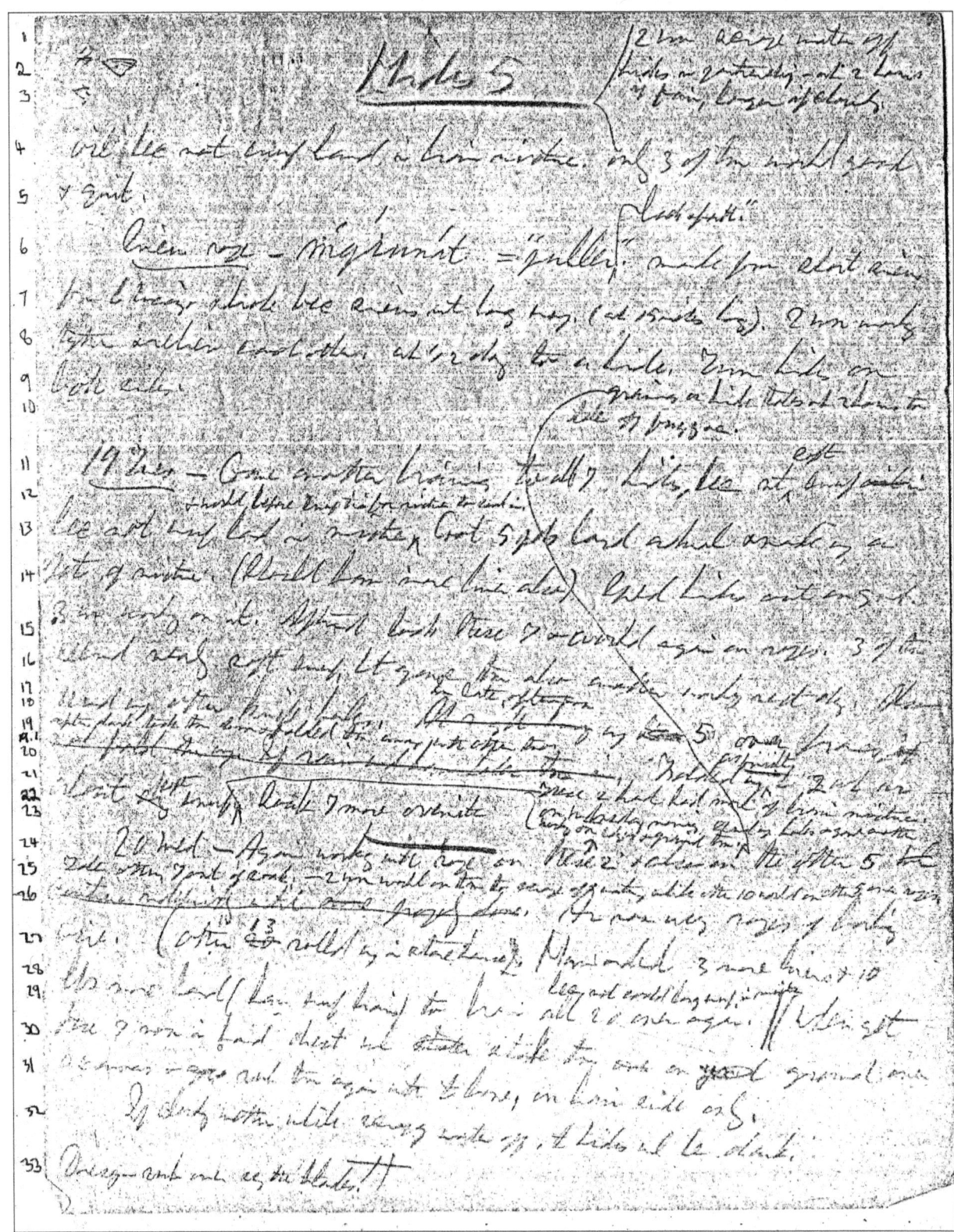

"Hides 5"

[1] 2 women scrape water off
[2] hides in partnership — at 2 hours
[3] if fair, longer if cloudy.
[4] [cont'd from page 4] oil because not enough lard in brain mixture. Only 3 of them worked good
[5] & quit   lack of [?]
[6]   Sinew rope = [Cheyenne word]   puller   made from short sinews
[7] from Chicago & broke because sinews not long enough (at 15 inches long). 2 women working
[8]   together & relieve each other. At ½ day to a hide.   Trim hides on
[9]   both sides
[10]   graining a hide takes at 2 hours to
[10]   take off fuzzy [?].
[11] **19th May Tuesday** – Give another braining to all 7 hides, because not soft enough
[12]   and worked before   enough time for mixture to soak in.
[13] because not enough lard in mixture.   Cook 5 quarts lard awhile & make up a
[14] pot of mixture.   (Should have more liver also)   Opened hides out on ground.
[15] 3 hours working on it. Afterward took these 7 & worked again on ropes. 3 of them
[16] worked nearly soft enough, but greasing them also makes working rest [of hides] okay. Also
[17]   in late afternoon [and]
[18] used up other knife [?].   At night hung up 5 over frames, [?]
[19] after dark took them down & folded them away   until after tomorrow
[19.1]   [erased text?]   (as finished)
[20]   Folded up 2 worked until [go to Line 22]
[21]   (These 2 had had more of brain mixture.)
[22] about soft enough   Soak 7 more overnight. on Wednesday morning, closed up holes & gave another
[23]   working on edges & grained them.
[24] **20th May Wednesday** – Again working with rope on these 2 and also on the other 5.
[25] Take other 7 out of soak. – 2 women worked on the to scrape off water, while other 10 worked on other
[26]   [text line out here]   And soon made ropes of baling [go to line 27]   5 over ropes
[27] wire. (other 13 rolled up in storehouse) "Man" added 3 more livers & 10 [go to line 29]
[28]   because not soaked long enough in mixture.
[29] pounds more lard (has sufficient brains) to brain all 20 over again   When get
[30] these 7 soon in lard [?] will stake them on ground over
[31] a canvas – [?] rub them again with thinning bone, on hair side only.
[32]   If cloudy weather while scraping water off, the hides will be dank.
[33] Dressing — rub over scythe blades. [new paragraph symbol]

= Hides 6

1 Wed 20 Oct — Can't get [illegible] Commander only 7 hides
2 [illegible] to 13 hides — [crossed out]
3 Thur 21 — Cloudy [illegible] [illegible] Broke all [illegible] with heat
4   [illegible] to draw 7 [illegible] 13 to draw
5 Fri 22 — [illegible] hot & [illegible] [illegible]
6 Sat 23 — [illegible] at [illegible] folded up. Left 13 other folded
7   [illegible] [illegible] [illegible]
8
9 Sun 24 — Spread out all 13 [illegible] day. At [illegible] put 6 to
10   [illegible] [illegible]
11 Mon 25 — [illegible] 6 mi [illegible], put [illegible] [illegible]
12   [illegible] W. Lewis, [illegible] & [illegible]. At nite folded up the 6
13   half dried to [illegible] again Tuesday. Bed [illegible] all things for. Put 6
14   of the remains & the [illegible]. Lewis & [illegible], Lee 2 [illegible] left this day.
15 Tues 26 — finally [illegible] the clouds & [illegible] [illegible] [illegible] [crossed out] [illegible] on
16   [illegible]
17 Wed 27 —
18 Thurs 28 — [illegible] 1½ [illegible] [illegible], left & [illegible] Lee this [illegible]
19   of [illegible] get [illegible] [illegible]. Can't [illegible] [illegible] just Mrs Joe &
20   [illegible] Mrs Boston to [illegible] — [illegible] [illegible]

"Hides 6"

[1] **Wednesday 20th [May]** – Can't get livers. Give another coating of lard.
[2] & brains to 13 hides. [scratched out text]
[3] **Thursday 21st** – Cloudy weather delayed. Took all until Saturday
[4] noon to dress 7. Leaving 13 to dress.
[5] **Friday 22nd** – Saturday afternoon had 7 hang out in frames; did no work.
[6] **Saturday 23rd** – noon Took them in until 7 pm, folded up. Left 13 others folded [go to Line 8]
[7] also grained them.
[8] up in storehouse.
[9] **Sunday 24th** – Opened out all 13 hides today. At night put 6 to
[10] soak overnight.
[11] **Monday 25th** – Worked 6 over ropes, & scythes, first scraping
[12] water off. Leave other 7 sunning. At night folded up the 6
[13] half dressed to work again Tuesday. Fold up all & bring in. Put 6
[14] of the remaining 7 to soak. Leaves 1 unsoaked because 2 women left this day.
[15] **Tuesday 26th** – finished working the above 6 & grained them by pegging on
[16] ground.
[17] **Wednesday 27th** – [no entry]
[18] **Thursday 28th** – Worked ½ day on remainder, left 1 unfinished because too hard,
[19] until get additional liver. Got 1 liver Thursday June 1st.
[20] Bring Mrs. B & 1 woman to finish. — Friday [June 2nd] start sewing.

Postscript

James Mooney's Cheyenne tipi hide tanning notes are as revealing of what the Cheyenne tanners — less than a dozen women — didn't do as what they did. Only experienced buckskin tanners like myself can understand what that means. In a very real sense, it's privileged information that we, as tanners, have earned the right to know and to act upon. But with that privilege comes the responsibility to share with others who also want to know, understand, and act upon. This is the underlying message of the Cheyenne women, joined by Mooney, that I have come away with. It has always been my way to credit those who've come before me as my teachers, whether I knew them personally or not, and whether they were alive or had passed on long before my time.

Technical notes

Technically, the Cheyenne women who "dressed" these 27 cow hides clearly sought to embed as much lard, brains, and liver into the raw skins as possible to render them flexible enough to trim, sew, and fashion into a tipi. However, based on the ingredients they requested and Mooney provided them with, it is equally clear that no Aldehyde tannage occurred until, on at least one occasion (at Darlington Indian Agency), the tipi was pitched and a wood fire introduced smoke into the interior. But smoke tannage was minimal based on my inspection of the tipi at the Field Museum in Chicago over 35 years ago. It is interesting that these tanners were adamant about the relative amounts of the ingredients used, and Mooney reflects this in his notes, particularly on page 2. I attribute this not to any tanning effect, but to render the untanned skins sufficiently flexible to manipulate in the rubbing stages.

Here and there (e.g., page 4) the tanners explain to Mooney the supreme importance of soaking hides. They tell him that the "old way" was to throw "hot water into open hide and [add] dry grass to retain water & often twisting them up with sticks so as to [express] water." But, Mooney is told by Mrs. B, "tubs are better." Mooney had supplied them with metal tubs large enough to hold one skin each for soaking, using rocks to hold them under the water.

It is also noteworthy that the Cheyenne tanners used domestic cow hides rather than bison. The latter would have been scarce at this point in time due to the "Great Buffalo Trade" that contributed heavily to the species near extinction from 25 million to less than 600 individuals by 1890. However, the challenges of "brain tanning" with domestic cow hides are no different than with bison. As I wrote in *Buckskin Tanner* (p.42):

> Bison and cattle are both members of the genera bovine (Bovinae, a sub-family of Bovidae), ungulates with cloven hooves. The fibers of their respective hides reticulate (cross each other like a net), and are, thus, less flexible than hides of the deer family, whose fibers are more striated and prone to stretching. Anyone who has "brain tanned" deer and attempted bison hides knows what I'm talking about. So, it was clear from the [tanning] industry's science, reticulated fibers simply stand in the way of brain tanning.

By "standing in the way," I mean the collagenous dermis of the bovine, even if "brained 'til the cows come home," cannot sufficiently relinquish its glued-tight reticulation when "rubbed" to become soft and flexible like deer skins do. As the soaked (hydrated) untanned fibers dry out, they simply "glue" back together again into rawhide. Unless, as the Cheyenne tanners demonstrated, the brains are supplemented with copious amounts of lard (rendered animal fat). The raw, untanned hide is then somewhat pliable, but nothing like the soft, stretchy — and equally untanned — deer buckskin most of us are familiar with today. Nevertheless, until I had touched the Cheyenne tipi at the Field Museum, I can say I had never seen nor felt anything like it before: a beautiful creamy white (from the lard) finish and clearly flexible enough to drape over a set of pitched tipi poles. But not tanned, and that much we now know with certainty.

Not to despair buckskin tanners! There is more to the story! What Mooney's notes also revealed is what the Cheyenne women showed him and he recorded, but clearly did not understand: it's what would have happened next had the tipi not been taken from them and put into storage at the Field Museum. It was the part of the "Mooney Code" I cracked that I had been looking for. "The secret," one could say, to Plains Indian bison hide tanning. That Mooney missed this did not surprise me because he, like other visitors to Indian villages before him who published their own observations of Indian tanning, was not a tanner. Mooney was clearly more focused on what the Cheyenne women were doing — than not doing — to actually fabricate the tipi. Since the finished tipi is what he and the Smithsonian and the Field Museum wanted — not tanned hides. Had historical events unfolded otherwise, Mooney and others would have learned how the Cheyenne (and other Plains Indian tanners) actually tanned their bison hides to render them soft enough to wear. My companion book, *Buckskin Tanner*, explains exactly what to do as I replicated the process. Tanners will be as surprised as I was to learn that there is no need to "thin" the hide at all — even the thickest bison bull hides — to achieve the desired end result.

In summary, what the Cheyenne tanners did 116 years ago to preserve a central part of their material culture for posterity was both remarkable and selfless. While many in academia since 1903 can point to James Mooney as a pioneering anthropologist and ethnographer, joined by a chorus of historians and museum archivists, is there one who could point to Mrs. Red Eagle, Mrs. B, or "old woman," as someone they had ever heard of? With a military garrison looming close by at Ft. Reno as a constant reminder to the Cheyenne and Arapahoe at the Darlington Agency of their violent subjugation, meaning to do as they're told or else, speaks volumes to a strong and admirable character to share that which an imposing nation had sought to dismantle less than a generation before. James Mooney understood this, and so people like myself — buckskin tanners — are eternally grateful that he could facilitate this important replication of one part of the Cheyenne "old way" so that we too can learn and pass it along a century later.

Image Credits

Covers
- Back: Cheyenne woman: Edward S. Curtis, 1930: Public Domain
- Back: Unknown Cheyenne artisan. Photo by John Bigelow Taylor. This model tipi, or a very similar one, is now on exhibit at the Toledo Museum of Art. December 2017, Public Domain
- Naturescape: neyro2008 © www.123rf.com
- Author image: Jill Willis
- See also James Mooney photo credit below (title page and p. 6).

Title page, p. 6
- Public domain: Unknown photographer – "James Mooney," *American Anthropologist*, Vol. 24, No. 2 (April–June 1922), p. 209

P. 7
- Above — "Rath & Wright's buffalo hide yard in 1878, showing 40,000 buffalo hides, Dodge City, Kansas." U.S. National Archives and Records Administration: Public Domain
- Below — Burton Historical Collection, Detroit Public Library. Photograph 1892 of a pile of American bison skulls waiting to be ground for fertilizer: Public Domain

P. 8
- A.A. Hyde Collection of William S. Soule Photographs at Wichita State University Archive: Public Domain

P. 14-26
- *Miscellaneous notes on the Cheyenne 1903-1906*. Manuscript 2213, National Anthropological Archives, Smithsonian Institution

P. 27
- Hide tipi. Watercolor on paper by Karl Bodmer (1809-1893) from his travel to the U.S. 1832-1834: Public Domain

P. 31

Jill Willis

Buckskin Tanner

. . . is about an ancient craft that provided clothing, shelter, and many utilitarian items in the lives of Native Americans, hunters, trappers, pioneers and others who once lived close to nature. An animal taken for food also provided these things. "How I tan today is based on what I learned from historical accounts, trial and error, Indians, other buckskinners like myself, and even the tanning industry. It's an artful craft worth mastering and passing on to posterity."

Order your copy signed by the author exclusively at:
www.NaturalWorldPublications.net

Perfect Bound and E-Books also available:
www.Amazon.com

About the Author

I've always been a maverick thinker and doer, never satisfied with life's limits as I've perceived them to be in the mainstream. For example, after leaving the U.S. Army in early 1970 with an honorable discharge, I joined other veterans in the antiwar movement in protest of the corporate "war for profits" in Vietnam and the average American's unwitting complicity. "No business as usual" was our mantra, and on many fronts the burgeoning protest movement confronted every institution across the country. As mounting numbers of dead and wounded were returned home, the entire nation began questioning and then demanding an end to the war. In 1975 President Nixon felt the hand of the movement and shut it down — the greatest military blunder in the history of the U.S. After that, we all went own separate ways.

My calling became "nature" and what we can learn as a species from our natural world, past and present. My books continue to tell my own story, where I've gone, what I've got myself into, with whom, and why. *Buckskin Tanner* is one chapter in that story.

www.ingramcontent.com/pod-product-compliance
Lightning Source LLC
Chambersburg PA
CBHW051355070526
44584CB00025B/3768